SOULFUL

NEESHANT SRIVASTAVA

Made with ♥ on the Notion Press Platform
www.notionpress.com

To my loved ones.

Contents

A BOOK

1. BEAUTIFUL WORLD

It's a beautiful world around us,
He is fair, tall and unlikely to thicken,
He walks around in youth and the girls gaze,
A young man and a world of takers,
Maybe a white girl, flawless and stunning,
In a the world of whites,
Plenty of hands and merry making on dark nights,
When the steam is all healing, all conquering,
The world around us has blurred and vanished,
The trees, lights of gold, the breeze, the Fall, fans for ease,
Amass and amass, it's your day in the sun,
Comfort and fun, and a glorious night,
That is yet to come and the eyes wander restless,
The spark of evil is upon us and we can get along,
No complains for the hell we have yearned for,
Just a smirk and the party of revellers inebriated,
You've qualified for an entry into this remarkable world,
Drink and drink until this body shall cease,
For no one knows anything that we don't know,
It's the same human frame and the same desires,
Let the young ones come along and experience,
An encounter with evil and easy ways to euphoria,
Cheat, deceit, fraud and worship, all in one lifetime,
A new morning and a new life all over again,
It's a beautiful world and don't ask why,

Those eyes wobble and hands tremble with fear,
Let's be done with the day and the night,
Look even the creator has taken the day off,
We don't want old and wrinkled and faceless,
Go for young, the heartthrob, the killer,
Be high again with your shooting arrow,
For this is a beautiful world.

2. BROKE OF ART

That boy or girl knows at three or eight,
A path so sure of,
In a dismissive world there will be thorns,
Blow aloud and silence those voices,
A talent is a rare gift of God,
A heart within seeks no rooms of sweat,
Or a place to hide and sharpen the machete,
It wants a total riddance of those dark walls,
That may not be seen by the prodigy,
It's twisted and twirled like a venomous snake,
Do not try to come close,
It shall blow your world away,
With the pounce of the deadliest fangs ever known,
A heart begging the artist to drop the art,
For there are urgent matters that need attention,
A total freedom from dark and allow surface,
Great illuminated walls of constant silver,
Is the greatest dream of an artist,
Then the art is art and completely soulful,
Don't let art follow the route of a merchant,
Let it flow aimlessly and paint the essence,
Don't let it be heard or aspire a dig,
Let those heavenly hands carry it like the breeze,
For it's the art that survives and not the artist,
Be a broke artist without chamfered walls,

To let the heart dance to glory, free from any venom,

There are no caravans of lights and song,

Celebrating the lips of monologue,

For the utterance of the sumptuous word,

It's just the divine that sits in the glorious heaven.

3. FALLING TO PIECES

This is the season of Fall, beware,
No leaves of colour,
No sun with a silk of crimson skies,
No images of a white Christmas with bells of Santa,
Please hold your masks tight,
There's a strong wave of anger building,
Like a great storm,
That is predicted to destroy anyone in sight,
Look, the future is clearer than the present,
And there's someone with a gun tonight,
Me thinks the law is ought to put us behind bars,
But we are very sure,
We have not committed any crime, please,
Young girls are moving on the streets,
With a pretence of a live cell phone on their ears,
They are just checking out the guys that pass by,
To see if someone fits the bill,
They have been decreed by stern parents,
To get married by May,
The mind has blown to pieces,
It is playing a catch me game,
It is throwing random balls in the air,
And each thought has a trigger of its own,
There's too much noise
And a toss of impudent eye balls,

Catching more than they should,

My health has ditched me,

It's breaking down too soon,

I think a cigarette or a swig might help,

Don't let into the city,

It's a mayhem beyond control,

Look at that young blood,

It already has an overworked mind,

Perhaps they are too eager for the season of Fall,

Human, anyone?

4. FOLLOW ME

There a voice in my youth – 'Follow me',
The boat a' creak and the crooked known,
That black heart and intentions to destroy,
A voice – 'Follow me' and I did,
How can love and hate survive together,
Is it possible that the love is hampered,
Lie down low, please, no questions,
A father in his invisible plans,
The boy in a cocoon cannot make out,
No breeze or a whisper from the outside,
The voice – 'Follow me', and I did,
Lie down low, please, no questions,
The manager of the store urged the lad,
'Stay, please, you can learn, don't go away',
The voice- 'Follow me', and I did,
Lie down low, please, no questions,
Lad a' marriage, his first, happy tidings,
Mother says, 'Sunny we gotta run over that bitch',
Walk in the opposite direction of logic,
Mother knows better, she save her child,
The voice- 'Follow me, and I did,
Lie down low, please, no questions,
'Sunny never do you compromise, you hear',
Lonely again, no graph to display,
Lord said- 'Follow me', and I did,

Lie down low, please, no questions,
There appeared heaven and end to sadness,
No one in sight but the Lord in conversation,
With a voice- 'Follow me', and I am,
Lie down low, no questions.

5. JUST A MAN

Don't ask me if I am a man of God,

Or,

If the Almighty is evident to my eyes,

Or,

Why I don't go near idols of Him in temples,

Or,

Why I'm caught in human webs and can't move,

Or,

Why my mind has been hushed and asked to kneel,

Or,

Why my mother assessed me as a great fool,

Or,

Why I break my bones for words said long ago,

Or,

Why my insanity has given way to sanity,

Or,

Why I write on walls that stand in the backwaters asleep,

Or,

Why I am ugly but still have a heart filled with love for all,

Or,

Why I am a great sinner and don't deserve God's whispers,

Or,

Why I was born to serve by killing myself and rising again,

Or,

Why I am the peculiar one and out of place,

Or,

Why I did what I did that no one else ever did,

Or,

Why I feel I am inches away from hell and eager to dive into it,

Or,

Why I struggled so hard to be lonely and yet be in bliss,

Take me away right now, O! Lord, I can't speak anymore,

After all I am just a man.

6. FESTIVAL SEASON

The festive season,

And those endless stalls with ladies,

What do we need for the grand puja,

Laces, diyas, cotton wicks, idols, and more,

For Ma Durga, Sri Ram, Chhatt puja,

Time for an exhaustive list of things we have not,

Troubled times and the auspicious season,

Let's light diyas, sound the tinkling bells, and sing,

It's a given that God shall fulfil all our wishes,

We don't ask for much, it's just peanuts, really,

Let there be magic and we be transported to heaven,

These offerings of gold, sweetmeat, shine on plates, laces,

Is for our dear Lord and have been accumulated with pain,

They don't deserve to be squandered on humans,

That lone house is always abuzz with prayer, song, dance,

They have found a way to talk to the Almighty,

Their strife has lasted longer than they expected,

They have been denied wealth, money, income,

They stand on one leg in a prayer to goddess Laxmi,

At the end of a prayer session,

They spew flowers to Ma Laxmi in anger,

For the lean season never ends,

They are the special holy ones sent by God,

So they believe,

It's the festive season, children,

Let's all forget what this is all about,
Just enjoy the music, vibe, women and lights,
And God shall fill us anyway.

7. I BELONG

I belong to that road of tears and laughter,

A miss here and breakdown there,

Lord, I have seen men of stone with lost feeling,

I don't like the sight of cold and barbarous men,

For I have been guilty of a grave crime,

And I have asked for forgiveness from my father,

Saying, 'How in the world did you disrespect your mother',

I suppose I died that very moment,

And carried my carcass far and long,

And wonder why my father of all men,

Chose to live that long with me as his follower and servant,

He's carrying the dead me and I don't hear anything,

Sometimes his eyes bent low as a respect,

To me the destroyer of happy and a grave sinner,

How could I make my lips to utter Thy Name,

For I never saw my father utter Thy Name,

Only a blue Gita by his table stood damp,

When my father sprinkled holy water on it each day,

And he did circle his bed for strength,

'Pardon me' as these words come out of a human,

That cannot find yet an appropriate word,

I was always far away from You,

As my father carried my death on his shoulders,

Urging me never to give up the game,

For there is a God within each one of us,

And I belong to this changing river,
Endowed with tears of my father and mother,
Hoping something out of a dead rock,
Here's to them in that I might have,
Found something here,
After the unending tide of ignorance,
That blinded me for ages,
That has given way to a clear path and more,
I belong to those two hearts that wept for me,
A proud son and longing to lie prostrate,
Before them in devotion.

8. LET'S PLAY

Ever since the world began, probably,

I am sure you love me, but I know you don't,

Can't you see my posture d'mask, I am your lover,

Look I am cross with you, please me, solve it,

You didn't have to say so much, dear,

For I know you love me, after all,

We are eternal lovers, just dish out all with the emotion,

You know that I don't care, but still, you love me,

Let's play that game, I hate and then love,

And you hate and then we make up,

Can you carry the thought that I hate you,

For you are a messiah and a saviour of souls,

And bla…bla…bla, just please me and give me all you have,

For I hate your ugly face,

What are you going to about it,

And still the greatness in me perhaps,

Lays down low for a failure that's you,

All's Ok if you did not know,

I was just playing that love game with you,

You and me, lovers and haters rolled in one,

For I don't see you going anywhere,

Stick to this game and maybe God intervenes,

And gives you what you do not deserve,

Polish me with words that speak high of me,

And I shall keep you as my slave till the end,

Pass that ball and I shall pass it back to you,
And then you pass it to me and I,
Again, with anger, dislike, hate, and love,
Will pass that back again,
This maker of verses is indeed the greatest villain,
But this time he let God decide,
Why their life is hell and they are headed there,
And his life an awakening,
With Him the charioteer and he the dead,
Into a great meadow he never saw or expected.

9. WALK TO THAT GARDEN

The word is out,
People that desire the utmost,
Frantically search for gurus,
This one and that one revered more,
Oh! That bag of tricks and powers match none,
Him I shall call my guru,
O! Holy one show me the way,
A long wait and the road to there never ends,
If man is clever, intelligent, skilful, then,
What about the force that created man,
What can a man do in so many years,
Where half the time he has to deal with others,
And there is no room for a personal touch,
He is looking at the growing crowd,
Knowing that he will find none,
That shall consider this inner journey,
And in ages and ages of wait,
Maybe someone appears on the horizon,
When He rubs his eyes in total disbelief,
He then prepares the battleground,
Where this promising warrior has to fight alone,
And there is a bright chance of him failing,
And he sends people and more people to make that happen,
This town of revel has learnt newer and spiteful games,

To disrobe and disturb the mind to the point of,
A great inner chaos,
That eventually leads to a complete human collapse,
And that bright star suddenly vanishes,
And He walks alone in that garden of His.

10. SYSTEM WE BELIEVE IN

You gave your life,

And those people have lost direction,

They are singing in the common choir,

They believed in a beautiful life,

And a complete fool could have missed that stanza,

A strong compelling force to all and more,

Riding higher and higher in the blood of youth,

While you got lost in the ghastly crowd,

Weaving alone in a corner,

No one to your beck and call,

No one to wipe your tears,

That you never let appear,

It is for my son that I must save,

He is blind and too far away from the wind,

My husband went away,

And his death he did choose,

Said we are one in a common cause,

Our son needs our help and we must,

She said in love did I die,

And I must die again,

Said I believe in the system,

Onlookers complained,

Said they cannot see it coming ever,

She says you may not have given yourself up ever,

I cannot make you out in your chiffon and bindi,
For I never seen any flesh or bones,
My husband the supreme,
And a walk on water,
I lost my shape a long time ago,
And this child needs me,
I walk on fire and can only see stars,
And those plastic flowers,
That shall blossom for ever,
I believe in the system,
And this child of mine shall know it too,
When he walks out of his daze,
So long little one, I must leave now,
Remember what mama told you,
Believe in the system,
And never expect the whirlwind,
Stay put like the day.

11. IT DOESN'T MATTER
(if you did not make it)

Do not expect the final goal,

Man in realm of manifestations,

A peek here and a sad regret,

For there was always something missing,

The greatest goal is the simplest of all,

That to be human even to the foe,

To carry an ocean of love within,

For extinguishing a fatalistic fire,

This one simple goal and man has failed,

Sing that song O! oarsman in the river,

Your life ended abruptly I know,

When you tried to save someone,

From the currents that took you away,

Do not wail for the life that passed you,

It doesn't matter if you did not make it,

Here's a new life and you are in august company,

Don't go near the water, please listen,

They shall save you from danger,

And never let you die,

You are in His hands and you must,

Show what's in your heart,

And let that pain decide how far you go,

You have travelled far, O! sailor of ages,
It doesn't matter if you did not make it.

12. THE WEIGHT

That lame man born in the black town,
With no face of delight or ponder to see,
A rather rude awakening of ordinary eyes,
A man that was not enough for a world in flight,
A man not man enough for a woman,
For he cried and cried not at his crutch,
But for those eyes that were deep in sadness,
Why then did he go so far,
When there were ways to inject life,
And be an indominable body of crush,
For those skinny ladies with perfect hourglasses,
When the colour is the rage for greater pleasure,
You fool, you ass, don't give up this beautiful opportunity,
And cry for something no one can see,
Don't be too sure of the road that does not exist,
Don't get under the skin and expect a life,
And be drowned in sorrow and insanity for life,
Don't ever think of carrying that weight, my son,
You shall never get there,
It's most unbecoming of a human,
Look they are in tears as if they really tried,
When every one knows where the fault lies,
But no one will admit but offer pithy lines,
As if they have the greatest soul and more,
They are trying to act noble when they know,

Where they failed and what went wrong, believe me,
Perhaps they are looking for greater fun, believe me,
They are all in flight and headed nowhere, my son,
Why then did He choose this lame man, O! dear,
Born in the black town and with no eyes of delight to see,
Can you really carry the weight, don't even try to,
Why do you have nothing at all except alms,
After years and years of carrying the heavy load,
Perhaps He thinks this man that is not a man,
Can and he must be the horse with blinkers,
Whipped and flogged until he died and is exhumed,
By His terse hands to carry the weight some more,
Till the very end,
That weight is too much for humanity.

13. TALKING TO WHOM

Where are you, my friend,

I cannot see you,

What do I do my heartfelt,

I just saw one rugged path with stones like wilderness,

No flowers to speak of then and in spring,

Why in the world did I attempt to walk through,

I was so lonely and even my shadow had left me,

No skies, no road, no stars, look I walked alone,

I couldn't say where this gloom would end,

And I had been pushed to the end of the queue,

And even further where not even animals roam,

I was walking along carrying this carcass,

My father and my mother had turned so quiet,

They said I was depressed,

And a host of others I never heard,

I was at the bottom of the abyss,

I needed help but had forgotten to ask,

I was dead but my pulse knocked at me,

Twenty-nine years and I heard a voice,

Come cheat on Me and get through,

And I still didn't know what I heard,

I was a catch to the evil and more,

They were putting ideas into my head,

And I did follow them like a zombie,

I was about to make the greatest fall,

And be smashed to a million pieces,

But I didn't until I saw Him ringing the bell,

Announcing the arrival of me, a somebody,

And the first thing, I decided to talk to you,

And looked into your eyes and what did I find,

Your eyes were aligned but you were a stranger now,

Whom am I talking to, my dearest,

You have childlike ideas and you are glistening,

To something unreal and lacking any ground,

Your roots are uprooted and you have drifted,

Into skies that are foreign that don't mean a thing,

To you and those foreign skies,

You are blind and cannot see your enslavement,

When the solution is as easy as that Maker,

Talks to me and fills me with simplicity,

Out of a road I followed in my backyard,

Don't show me the seven seas,

I just need a six-foot space to sleep,

I am sorry I don't know you anymore,

While the Maker is planning my day ahead,

And a simple walk to the world of my dreams,

And I am just a traveller in time,

With a grand realization that life has a meaning.

14. TWO FOR COMPANY

Where have these people come from,
Out on the streets and every corner of this earth,
Just moving and making a restless sound,
Unceasing, longing for company and thrill of friends,
Selling themselves cheap to monsters of gaze,
A touch and an eye for the sore in their lives,
Alone will be a disaster for the deep devil within them,
That will not cease to give evil ideas and dirty schemes,
The self is too dark and they may sink into a lack of motion,
And clog the mind into waves of the insane, paranoid,
Let it be a small place to sit in a quiet restaurant,
Surrounded by people that seem to have a purpose in their eyes,
For it is true that they must keep moving, always,
They cannot bear the thought of sitting alone,
A sea of silence is most uninviting and torturous,
They are happy to be captive to other humans,
It is but natural for them,
To carry a strong hatred for these other humans,
And to plan a downfall of these other humans,
If they happened to above their own category and status,
Thus engender a life of pick and catch,
Make friends, be jovial,
They are all there to help them,
And they will not let them be alone,
Never has it then happened in centuries,

For a man or a woman to emerge from the crowd,

And for whom every moment is priceless,

Every wind, every sound, every number, every thought,

Is vital as they live each day in a beautiful world,

Where every tick of the clock is an opportunity,

To see more than what eyes will ever see,

To grow into a magnificent tree with great roots,

And a generous sprinkling of the leaves,

The branches of which are dressed by sweet, colourful birds,

Different in different seasons and in huge numbers,

To sing a song so free and without any danger,

In celebration of a victory called life,

Two for company is what we will ever need,

If not then we have lost the most precious thing we had,

And the impoverished lot shall loiter in jungles,

Of lust and the dark cloud of negative thoughts,

That shall hang over them forever and never pour,

For they have been reduced to less than animals.

15. KITE'S FLYING HIGH

This kite is flying high,
Don't pass it tales of long ago,
Of the wrong that was done,
And the way it was done,
That great rub along congested pathways,
When it was stuck and did not move an inch,
When the heat and sweat ran through its veins, a company to,
Those retarded brains with a mind of a stagnant mule,
Who never ever walked a mile in sixty,
And knew not better that being bonded slaves,
In such a cacophony accept it as a life,
Like they had done their 'Dharma' in this their 'Karma',
In a land we call hell,
Couldn't want more than the soaring kite, please,
Let me be known as a frail human, Sir,
For I do not possess more than what You gave me,
And when You decided to keep shut,
In those times that were beyond control,
For me to know and react to what was happening,
My dear God, it's true that I did fight in those times,
But I am not a crusader with a voice,
I am a dumb and deaf dummy,
That stood in the corner without knowing what hurt,
Please don't give me the nitty-gritty,

Of those tough times when I'd rather be dead,

And of how I broke loose with those tight fetters,

Around my neck and my midriff, and those anklets of bondage,

I know not the exact depth of my pain, I agree,

And I also know that You know,

That any kind of revelation will not stutter me,

And change the way I treat them with kind eyes,

And how I now love every soul,

I am so indebted to You, perhaps You know not,

I am a grain of dust that happened to fly,

Let me rather resemble the kite,

That has taken to the high skies,

I know what I know, and I really do know,

The depths are just a little stretch of my conclusion,

I now sing in peace and glory,

In grace to those hands that made me fly,

That gave me a reason to survive,

And prayed this kite to fly like I do,

To the skies above the skies and even higher,

To their delight and remnants of soggy eyes,

My greatest fortune, God bless those hands,

Let me be among the high and very high,

I don't see anything anymore.

16. POETRY THE DIVIDING LINE

Poetry is the harsh line,

That divides life from non-existence,

Poetry is esoteric, talking of the higher,

It is abstract art or closely a drop of scenery on canvas,

It will make no sense and shall pass the eyes,

Poetry is on a journey,

It's getting farther and farther away from the majority,

In the genesis of a new age,

When God's Hands have sought a degradation,

That music is coming to an end,

It died with the American pie*,

The age of darkness hence,

Cannot feel the simple and the innocent,

With words off those that can break bondage of ages,

It's no time for freedom,

Let's lie low, there's too much of noise,

Faithful sons, truthful sons, honest sons,

That will recover the great debt,

Of fathers and mothers, and the guru,

Have gone away,

Poetry is of the heart, the soul,

And music is for the free-flowing soul,

An age of comfort and no pain,

Cannot elicit a word that talks of sacrifices,

And the loss for some gain and vice versa,

Poetry is a cruel act,

With a clear diving line,

It's knocking off the great minds,

That run on logic,

Let's breath softly,

Someone is not happy here.

*Popular song written and sung by Don Mclean

17. HAVE NO NAME

I am the wind,
I have no name,
My life a creaking boat of old wood,
The gaps too many and I with two hands,
Trying to fill in with burnt wood,
It holds for a while but gives in,
I have sailed far away from the village,
I only hear the creaking sound,
And the broken oar too old to push the water,
I am alone and never felt so excited,
I don't know why but I have a deep frown,
I am trying to catch something the Master said,
I am deep down buried in the mud,
I am a servant to my gracious Master,
I have left my family and friends,
My Master says it's my new life,
But it's not clear why I still stay,
He says I have accomplished the day,
And its time to rest my bones,
Mention of a maiden and I am crestfallen,
I sometimes cry alone and I know why,
She might have missed my boat,
And still lingers in the village,
I am not in a hurry to leave,
I stand in alertness to my next order,

And I can keep promises, my Master knows,

My name was buried the day I saw,

My father in pain,

I hear voices and see faces now,

My Master is very kind to me.

18. IT'S NOT IN DYING

There a lightning fell on a good heart,

He could not take it anymore,

Said the people are thick skinned,

Rigor mortis the paper read,

One true heart and unbearable heat,

There a soft boy and his mind of alarms,

Someone somewhere has threatened his end,

To survive would be to give in to the game,

There someone stands defeated on the edge,

Of a tall sky scraper and the wind cannot stop the fall,

What then is the road we must take,

Where do we go and what do we do,

Whom do we listen to and whom to abide by,

A lesser human is not permissible to the heart,

To walk like weak men and give into the darkness,

To act as someone else and kill within,

Is not the world we dream of,

When every moment is a moment of doubt,

Every step is taken singly,

No one's umbrella is above us,

And more often than not life is a disaster,

For we all have the fear of the end,

We cannot sit and pour our hearts to our work,

What if we have all that we want,

When our wants seem to be unreal and misleading,

How can we crack the final deal,

And be convinced of a better life after this,

It's not in dying that this maze can be conquered,

It is in the 'great fight' in the battlefield of life,

Seeking the light within like little children in the dark,

When things go out of hand,

But never settling for less than a human being,

Of strength, dignity, honesty and a heart of pure love,

For He cannot be the cruel Master, forever,

We are His special guests,

And we deserve the gifts of the Holy,

Burn now if you can,

A great day is about to dawn.

19. TYRANNY

There stands a tyrant,
There's a conspiracy being hatched,
That one must be brought down,
Who has a right to take lives,
In ways barbaric never heard before,
To shoot differently each time for the same red,
God is above us and we must notice,
His manifestations and His ways,
We must hear the Divine, we must,
For we are but His own frame,
Don't take a step without the divine,
He is flowing through us and we,
Are but His own medium,
Can you not feel the love, O! Holy man,
He's a wink away in your prayer room,
Don't you hear Him at all, O! precious,
When He cannot understand,
Why should we have hatred for others,
When He made this indelible human chain,
And felt proud of this great human family,
And He came several times to our land to save us,
Perplexed to find that we are so close,
Yet do not cross over for a silly thing,
Why come again O! humanity to this space,
Let God create a greater world for us,

And all of us children feel the magic of love,
Words that are scattered and spilled all over,
Are not fiction but a reality of life,
They are what we should be and can be,
Don't waste this opportunity, O! traveller,
It may not come again.

20. GO ANALOG

Where are you headed, O! technology man,
The map is ready to a push button reality,
We have reached a new high in our experiments,
We have made living a two-minute game,
The phone is your gateway to paradise,
Endless possibilities and you shall never starve,
Companies on the palm of twelve-year-olds,
Life amassed before the first chapter itself,
Don't ask where you are headed,
Your parents were too analog for your comfort,
They have stupid things like truth and honesty,
On their old lips,
They are not with the times, like they never were,
Why do you act churlish after amassing 'your' wealth,
Why are you so 'empty' and not like those past stalwarts,
What is missing in your life,
Why are you lost in a place called 'nowhere',
Where are you going, my dear children,
Why do you have anxiety attacks, and hypertension,
Felt by people above fifty in the past,
Watch where you are going while on the road,
Something might come unnoticed and slam you to the ground,
Throw away those gruesome tentacles growing around you,
They will not let you breathe, my friend,
Pick up a pen and clean sheet of paper,

Switch to analog before its too late.